A to Z

Active Learning Strategies
to support Spiritual and Moral Development

Joyce Mackley and Pamela Draycott

© Christian Education Movement 2000

ISBN: 1–85100–138–7

Introduction

This book describes active learning strategies which can be used across the curriculum but it focuses particularly on the spiritual and moral aspects of the curriculum and it has been compiled by a group of religious education specialists. So what is the connection between active learning, spiritual and moral education and RE?

FIVE PROPOSITIONS

1 **The whole purpose of education is to foster the personal growth of children – to help them to realise their human potential**

2 **The whole curriculum should support this aim**

3 **Spiritual and moral development relates particularly to this aim, and should pervade the whole curriculum**

4 **Religious education has a particular role within spiritual and moral education**

5 **In promoting personal growth, the processes of education are as important as the content**

Realising Human Potential

It is very easy amidst the current flood of government initiatives with their vocabulary of assessment, attainment, outcomes, competencies, levels and so on to forget that education is not ultimately about subjects and standards but about children and young people. No education system is worthy of the name if it does not help children to ask the question what it means to be human and to realise their human potential.

It is not always immediately obvious that this is what education is about. The school curriculum, with its emphasis on the acquisition of knowledge and understanding within certain traditional fields of human enquiry – literature, the arts, history, geography, the sciences, mathematics and so on, can easily obscure the fact that personal development is the true objective, not knowledge, or even understanding, for its own sake. A key element in realising human potential is awareness of oneself and the ability to relate to that self, to others, to the world, and perhaps to a transcendent reality. How much space does our subject-oriented content-laden curriculum allow for that essential process of self-discovery which enables us to relate – the essence of being human? And how do our methods of teaching relate to that fundamental aim?

The Whole Curriculum

These questions might seem to suggest that we need to rethink the whole of our education system, but this would be to underestimate the power of the traditional curriculum to promote personal growth if it is used to that end. The creation of literature is a fundamentally human activity, engaging as it does the power of an author to enter into other people's experiences and to convey their thoughts and feelings. At the other end of the educational spectrum (or so it would seem on a traditional view) mathematics, which is essentially a search for patterns and order, is equally a characteristic human activity. The problem lies not so much in the curriculum subjects as such but the way in which they are viewed both by teachers and by pupils under the pressures of a society which demands measurable performance. Traditional subject disciplines can be 'recovered' for their true educational purpose by the use of teaching strategies which help pupils to learn about themselves as well as absorbing the heritage of those who have gone before them in a particular educational discipline.

Spiritual and Moral

Viewed cynically, the current debate about spiritual, moral, social and cultural development may be seen as a panic response to a perceived breakdown of traditional values as evidenced by football hooliganism, rising levels of violent crime, high levels of divorce contributing to an increasing incidence of single-parent families and so on. More positively it can be viewed as a belated recognition that a subject-oriented content-laden curriculum can all too easily leave untouched precisely those issues and those experiences which contribute most to personal growth. Whatever the political motivation for the current concern with the 'spiritual' and 'moral', teachers should accept it gratefully as an opportunity and an encouragement to put questions about what it means to realise human potential at the centre of all areas of education.

Religious Education

It has rightly been stated that spiritual and moral development is not to be equated with religious education as if religious education were the only subject which had human development as its aim. That pupils should grow in their understanding of what it means to be human should be the aim of every teacher in every subject. Nevertheless RE is particularly well placed to pursue such an aim because it offers pupils the opportunity to look thorough the 'windows' of traditional faiths and see their visions of what a human life signifies. But RE, like every other subject, has to avoid falling into the trap of supposing that it is sufficient to tell pupils what other people think and feel without giving them any space to ask themselves what they think and feel. Knowledge and understanding of religious beliefs and practices is a necessary but not a sufficient condition in itself for real education to take place. It is not even enough to learn 'from' religions as well as 'about' them if this 'learning from' is not personally relevant – if it does not illuminate what it means to be human for me.

The Processes of Education

All of this suggests that we need to pay rather less attention to the content of the curriculum and more to the processes by which pupils learn. We need to ask ourselves what processes are most likely to promote self-discovery and develop pupils' capacity to relate to themselves and to others. Active learning strategies are particularly effective in this area, reaching the parts of pupils' personalities which other methods might not. Even a cursory glance at the A to Z listing which follows may suggest that active learning strategies can be effective in helping pupils to:

- affirm the worth of other pupils as human beings;
- enter into another person's problems;
- establish the range and strength of views and opinions on a given topic within the group;
- express moods and feelings;
- establish the group's basic values and put them in order of priority;
- develop listening and communication skills;
- explore methods of conflict resolution;
- develop reasoned arguments;
- understand what other people might be feeling;
- reflect on their own experiences;
- discover the importance of things that money can't buy;
- make the connection between beliefs, attitudes and actions;
- learn to work co-operatively with others;
- consider the personal qualities they think most desirable;
- learn to pay close attention to the world around us and to other people;
- confront fears and anxieties;
- trust other pupils;
- explore the questions to which there are no answers;
- learn how to make a stranger feel comfortable.

All of these are vital steps in the process of developing human potential. Some activities are most appropriate for use in curriculum time which has been specifically set aside for personal development. Others can be used as techniques within a wide variety of curriculum subjects. Where examples are related to a particular curriculum area it is mostly religious education but teachers from other subject areas can readily adapt them. And if you ever feel worried that you are not giving your pupils enough 'content', look at the list above and think what you are giving them that really matters.

MORE ABOUT ACTIVE LEARNING

Theoretical Perspectives

The terms 'active learning', 'experiential learning' and sometimes 'hands-on learning' may be used interchangeably to encompass those curriculum experiences which focus on active and participatory learning. 'Learning by doing' is a theme that many educators have stressed since John Dewey argued in the 1930s that children must be engaged in an active quest for learning and new ideas. Few teachers are unaware of the cognitive development work of Jean Piaget and the fact that he stressed the need for 'concrete operations' in early childhood. Some, however, incorrectly assume that active learning is therefore important only in the pre-school years and the early years of school. Piaget made it clear that 'experience is always necessary for intellectual development … the subject must be active … '. He also concluded that 'knowledge arises neither from objects nor the child but from interactions between the child and the objects.' This is as true at the age of sixteen as it is at six; indeed with the present emphasis on life-long learning, one could say at sixty. As the old adage puts it:

> I hear, I forget
> I see, I remember
> I do, I understand.

What Counts as Active Learning?

Active learning can be defined as learning which involves pupils in doing things and thinking about (and consequently learning from) the things that they are doing.

Some general characteristics of active learning are as follows:

- Pupils are involved in more than listening to the teacher. They are actively engaged in a range of activities (for example, reading, writing, the creative arts, discussing, playing games, researching, presenting).
- There is an emphasis on co-operation and collaboration. The sharing of ideas and learning from each other and the sharing of responsibility is important.
- There is less emphasis on transmitting information and more on developing pupils' skills as a way of promoting academic and personal development and achievement. Active participation involves pupils in higher-order thinking (such as analysis, synthesis and evaluation).
- There is an emphasis on pupils exploring their own attitudes and values and taking responsibility for their own learning.
- The teacher's role is to facilitate learning, not to be the arbiter of all knowledge and understanding but to empower pupils to take control of their own learning.

Active Learning and the Teacher

In using active learning strategies, teachers do not abdicate their responsibility to teach. They need to:

- have clear learning objectives for the activities that they wish their pupils to take part in;
- organise the physical learning environment (classroom, library, visit out of school, range of resources and so on) in ways which promote the active involvement of their pupils;
- establish a climate for interaction (trust, co-operation, discipline, frameworks for routines and ways of working);
- intervene appropriately to encourage and deepen learning (review work so far, probe through questioning, set further tasks and so on);
- monitor learning (self, peer and teacher assessment are all important in active learning) and plan for further activities which both consolidate and extend learning.

Moving towards the regular use of active learning strategies can create anxiety in teachers because it requires a different understanding of the teaching role. Active learning defines the role of the teacher as facilitator rather than fount of all knowledge. It is in some respects a less secure mode of teaching because the outcomes are less predictable. At the same time it is liberating to be freed from the necessity of appearing omniscient. It frees teachers to become learners alongside their pupils.

A key to successful active learning, as in all teaching and learning situations, is careful planning. Instructions need to be clear and problems anticipated. Be prepared to make appropriate interventions, posing open-ended and extending questions. Be prepared to introduce new methods gradually. It would not be wise to attempt a 20-minute guided visualisation without trying some shorter reflective exercises first. Aim for progression in learning activities as well as in curriculum content. As far as possible ensure that the environment is appropriate to the activity by a suitable arrangement of furniture, the provision of a visual focus or whatever. The context can be a key factor in the success or failure of an active learning exercise.

Active learning strategies do not always work with every group and in every situation. Do not be discouraged if active learning strategies produce occasional disasters. An activity which fails to achieve its intended purpose may be a useful learning experience nevertheless, especially if it is possible to discuss the reasons why it failed with the pupils. Remember that traditional teaching methods don't always work either, though it may be less obvious when they fail. It is helpful if other teachers in your school are also trying to introduce more active learning so that you can encourage and learn from one another.

THE TEACHING AND LEARNING PROCESS

Active learning methods, however effective, are only one weapon in an armoury of teaching techniques. They will take their place in a wider teaching and learning process. It is important to pay attention to this wider context as well. The model suggested here has been developed in the context of religious education and spiritual development but is certainly applicable across that broad area of the curriculum which comes under the umbrella heading of the Humanities.

Good religious education engages learners in a process whereby they pursue their personal search for meaning in the context of questions raised by shared experience of the human race and the insights offered by major world faiths. This process has four main aspects: engaging, exploring, expressing and responding.

Engaging

Grounding teaching and learning in authentic life experience is vital if pupils are to be actively engaged and involved in their learning. Starting from lived experience is, of course, good educational practice – but particularly essential in RE. Too often RE has been reduced to teaching about religion in a sociological or phenomenological way – often leaving pupils with the feeling that religion is odd or alien, bizarre or belonging to the past. If religious teaching is to come alive to pupils, and actually stimulate deeper questions about their own life and purpose, we need to ground lessons in real experience – preferably that related to pupils themselves.

Carefully chosen stimulus materials and active learning strategies, if sensitively handled, open up pupils' thinking, acting as 'lift off points to learning'. The use of evocative stories, case studies, drama and role-play activities, an inspiring visit or visitor, will all encourage reflection on personal beliefs and values, stimulating deeper questions of meaning and purpose.

Exploring

This enables pupils to research and explore the questions raised by means of a variety of activities and by reference (in the case of RE) to the teachings of world faiths, taking account of syllabus requirements. Pupils should develop appropriate skills for exploring religions and life experiences and for responding personally to their exploration in a variety of ways, including the development of positive attitudes. A wide variety of tasks is needed to provide all pupils with the opportunity to do well and to develop knowledge, understanding and personal insight. Exploration includes encouraging pupils to look for more than meets the eye, to explore their own insights, and should include activities which help develop awareness ('that long slow looking that brings engagement with something other than ourselves'). Such awareness can be developed through: experiential and reflective activities such as stilling, relaxation and visualisation; the engagement of the senses – sight, sound, touch, taste and smell; the use of the expressive arts – activities, such as art, poetry, music, drama and dance, which engage pupils' imaginative and creative capacities. All these provide a practical and enjoyable way of encouraging pupils to explore and express their own feelings, beliefs and insights.

Expressing

Pupils need to be helped to find a language – not necessarily in words – to express their experience, learning and insight. The creative and expressive arts such as art, poetry, music, dance and drama engage pupils' imaginative and creative capacities and encourage them to explore and express deeper insights and feelings.

Responding

Response is the final outcome of the learning – it is the developing recognition of personal beliefs, values and attitudes, and may lead to significant attitude and behaviour changes emerging over time (often long-term). If there is no response we have to ask ourselves what we are doing.

FURTHER READING FROM CEM PUBLICATIONS

See *The Agreed Syllabus for Religious Education* for a more detailed exposition of the view of religious education and spiritual development which underlies this work. Designed as guidance for Agreed Syllabus Conferences, this contains a clear exposition of the nature of RE as a subject which must engage pupils in personal search related to human experience as well as knowledge of world faiths.

A Teacher's Handbook of Religious Education has a section on The Contribution of RE to Personal Development (pages 8–10) and pages 33–35 deal with Skills in RE and Attitudes in RE. Page 32 sets RE within the context of education as a whole.

Looking Inwards – Looking Outwards offers many active learning strategies applied to a particular project for spiritual and moral development. It includes a teacher's book and a set of pupil activity sheets as well as a pupil book.

Dilemmas and Decisions offers forty-eight games to help pupils wrestle with situations of moral ambiguity relating to eight areas of human experience. This and the previous publication are both designed with secondary pupils in mind but many of the activities can be adapted for use in primary schools.

The parallel series of books, **Primary RE in Practice** and **Secondary RE in Practice** exemplify the process model described here and illustrated diagrammatically below. Four titles have so far been published in each series: *Is It Fair?*, *What Matters? Finding the Real Me* and *Why Do People Suffer?*

Further details of all these publications may be obtained from CEM, Royal Buildings, Victoria Street, Derby, DE1 1GW, Tel: 01332 296655, Fax: 01332 343253, Email: cem@cem.org.uk

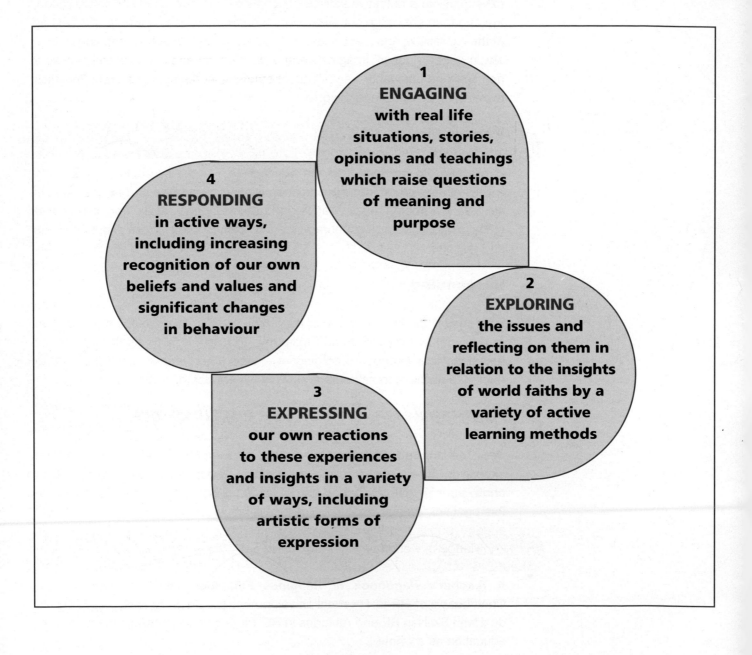

1
ENGAGING
with real life situations, stories, opinions and teachings which raise questions of meaning and purpose

4
RESPONDING
in active ways, including increasing recognition of our own beliefs and values and significant changes in behaviour

2
EXPLORING
the issues and reflecting on them in relation to the insights of world faiths by a variety of active learning methods

3
EXPRESSING
our own reactions to these experiences and insights in a variety of ways, including artistic forms of expression

Affirmation Exercise

Number pupils 1-30 (or whatever depending on the number in the group). Each pupil is given a sheet of paper and asked to write his or her name on the top line. The papers are passed to the next person (1 to 2; 2 to 3 and so on) who then writes a positive comment about the person on the *bottom* line. He or she folds the sheet up to hide the comment and passes it on to the next person. This continues around the room until everyone has his or her own sheet back.

This is useful for introducing themes relating to relationships; sensitivity toward the feelings of others; the value of personal affirmation; the value of 'unique' individuals, for example the Christian concept that all are created in the image of God and precious to God.

Note

This exercise needs careful preparation to highlight the importance of honesty and sensitivity towards the feelings of others. It works best in a group in which there is trust and co-operation.

Agony Aunts

Pupils will be familiar with the problem pages of teenage magazines. Writing and responding to letters of this type can be a way of encouraging pupils to reflect on their own and others' worries, thoughts, feelings, needs and so on.

An example might be: 'Dear ..., I am a Hindu and have met a really nice boy at school. He's asked me to go to the end of year disco with him. He's not a Hindu and I don't think that my parents would let me go with him. I'm 15. What should I do?'

Variation

Listening skills can be developed through telephone helpline improvisations.

Agenda-setting

Devise an agenda of questions for small discussion groups, taking care to challenge pupils to address all the key aspects of the topic. These can also be used to guide research and enquiry outside the classroom.

Agree/Disagree

This is useful as an opening gambit to a lesson or series of lessons.

Controversial statements are used to stimulate interest in the lesson content. Pupils who disagree with the statement move to one side of the room, those who agree move to the other. A continuation of this would be for pupils to form themselves into pairs or small groups with those on the same side to work out their argument for supporting their position on the issue.

Note

Depending on the topic, this exercise may reveal strong feelings and entrenched prejudices but that is part of the reason for doing it – to establish where the pupils are starting from and the scale of the task ahead if they are to be persuaded to give serious consideration to alternative viewpoints. (See also 'I Believe' under the entry on Discussion Groups)

Analysing a Problem

This is a useful method of involving pupils in consideration of a problem which may have occurred in school or outside in society. It is a strategy which takes the pupils' insights and perspectives seriously, and encourages them to take an active role in the resolution of the problem.

Discussion groups are formed (see entry on Discussion Groups) and the following questions are addressed:

- What is the problem?
- Who does it affect?
- Where, when and why does it happen?
- How could it be tackled?
- What is the best way forward?
- Who will take action?
- How will the action be monitored and reviewed?

Art Work

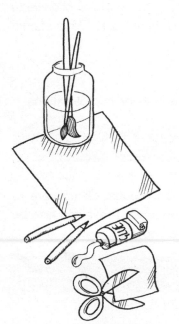

This can take various forms: collage, freehand drawing, sculpture, printing and so on. (See also separate entries on Body Sculpture, Collage and Collage Continuum) Art work can be very useful for displaying concepts and ideas along with written work, as well as allowing self-expression and communication for those who find other areas of communication difficult. The following examples are only suggestions for areas in which artwork can be effective.

Exploring change, death and rebirth

Use natural materials such as a branch of a tree or a flower stem to create a natural collage. Encourage pupils to express reflectively their own understanding of change, death and rebirth using the branch arranged on a sheet of sugar paper.

Exploring brokenness in human relations

This can cover such areas as remorse, confession, forgiveness and reconciliation. Again natural objects can be used imaginatively and very effectively to express emotions in these areas.

Colours

Used to express feelings and insights stimulated by story or music. For example, expressing the events of the Day of Pentecost; the Exodus crossing of the Red Sea; responses to music – joy in creation; incarnation; celebration; praise.

Wall Murals

What is a human being? Good and evil. Hope for the future.

Masks

For ritual use or to express emotion.

Display

Rich world, poor world. God's world.

Artefacts

These provide a wealth of material for pupils to be actively engaged with but they must always be treated with respect because of their significance to the faith traditions concerned. Some ways of using artefacts actively are offered below.

A mystery bag

A cloth bag with a question mark on it and a draw string top can be purchased or made. An artefact such as a chalice could be placed in the bag and the bag passed around the group. Pupils are asked to feel it carefully and to guess what it is and how it might be used.

Christian ways of praying

You will need two prayer books, two icons and two rosaries. Divide the class into six groups (think about whether the groups are to be random, friendship, ability). Two groups focus on an icon, two on the rosary prayer beads and two on a prayer book. Each group then explores the artefact – what it is, what it is made of, what it is used for, how it is used and how that use reflects Christian belief about prayer. One each of the icon, rosary and prayer book groups report back to their half of the class.

Variation

Use an icon, rosary and prayer book as a focal point on a table covered with a plain, pale-coloured cloth and with a small bowl of flowers and a candle on it. The table is set up in the centre of the room, with pupils sat around it, in silence. They are asked to look at the table and to reflect on the items. After a few minutes the artefacts are moved to three separate points in the classroom (each with room for pupils to sit around) and the pupils choose to go to sit around the artefact that interested them most. They then do a close observational drawing of it in the middle of a large piece of paper. On completion of the drawing they begin to find out more about the item and its use, using the rest of the sheet to present information about and responses to the artefact.

Note

The way in which the artefacts are used in this exercise can be adapted to relate to artefacts from other faith traditions or other themes within religion.

Simulation of a shrine

Set up in the classroom a simulation of a shrine used for worship (for example, a Buddhist or Hindu shrine) using the appropriate artefacts. Invite a Buddhist or Hindu into the class to talk about their shrine at home. Pupils look carefully at the shrine, listen to the visitor speaking about his or her worship and then write a short poem or piece of prose explaining their own attitudes to worship.

Awe and Wonder

A Mobius strip is a visual aid for breaking down expectations and stimulating a touch of awe, wonder and mystery. Make a long strip of paper by cutting an A4 sheet into three length-wise and joining the ends. Hold as if to make a cylinder, then put in a half twist (180°) and stick together.

How many sides has it got? Draw a line down the middle and find out. How many edges has it? Make a point on the edge and run your fingernail around it. A one-sided, one-edged piece of paper! Now cut along the line you drew down the middle of the paper. What do you expect to get?

What might this tell us about the way religion sees the world?

B Balloon Debate

Pupils imagine that they are crossing an ocean or desert in a hot air balloon with a range of different people (for example brain surgeon, industrialist, teacher) as their companions. Half way across the gas supply runs out and they are forced to make decisions about which of their companions should be thrown out in order for the balloon to stay aloft. This 'values clarification' exercise can be adapted and developed in a number of ways. The contents of the balloon can be objects or abstract values rather than people, for example.

Variation
Blow up a balloon to represent each person in the basket. Write the name and skill or attitude on each – for example Bill the Brain Surgeon, Mike the Materialist. Burst the balloon as the person is thrown out.

Body Sculpture

This is an active way of focusing pupils' thinking on the outward expression of inner feelings or attitudes – for example, love, anger, hatred – as expressed by a narrative, text, poem, video scene or whatever.

Pupils are paired. One takes on the role of the sculptor, the other the 'clay'. The sculptors 'mould' their partners to express the emotions or feelings they have 'picked up' from the stimulus material. Other pupils guess what inner feeling is being expressed. Photographing these could provide a useful starting point for discussion with other groups or make an interesting wall display.

Variation: Human Tableau
Divide the group into **A**s and **B**s. Explain that **A**s will take the active role first and the **B**s will be observers. Then the roles will be swapped. Form the **A**s into groups of 3–4 and give each a card telling them the theme. Groups then form living sculptures to depict the theme. Observers have to guess what the theme for each tableau is. The **A**s then become observers as the **B**s create the sculptures.

This technique could also be used to create a living sculpture of part of a story or incident, the emphasis being not only on what happened in the story but the feelings or emotions engendered by it. Suitable themes include: 'It's unfair'; jealousy; anger; success; fear; feeling loved; justice; peace; forgiveness.

Brainstorming

This is a useful activity for:

- establishing existing knowledge and understanding;
- generating new ideas;
- sorting ideas.

It can be used individually, in small groups or for the whole class.

A key word or topic is selected; pupils list as many ideas as they can think of relating to it. No comment is made at this stage, the object being to 'get down' as many ideas as possible in as short a time as possible. On completion of the brainstorm, discussion – in pairs, groups or whole class – enables the ideas and issues identified to be sorted and prioritised and further thoughts and ideas sought as appropriate. Key issues for further research and discussion should also be identified. (See also Discussion Groups)

Buzz Groups

Invite members of the class to spend a short time (2–3 minutes) talking to one or two people nearby about a specific topic or a reaction to something they have just seen or heard (for example input from a speaker or from an audio or video tape). It should be kept short and snappy to catch first reactions without getting involved in a full discussion. This method is useful for focusing attention on key points and issues.

Collage

Using newspapers or colour supplements, pupils produce a collage on a given theme, for example, evil, crucifixion, love. Scissors are not always required as the act of tearing can be part of the process, and the rough edges symbolic.

Collage Continuum

This is a useful device for exploring issues which can be expressed in terms of a continuum between two opposites, for example good and evil, peace and war, love and hate, justice and injustice.

Groups work together on a large piece of paper. Explain that one corner of the paper represents (for example) evil and the opposite corner represents good. The object of the exercise is for the group to work together to create a collage depicting a continuum or journey from the negative to the positive, using pictures, colours, symbols, words torn or cut out of magazines. The images should express the group's ideas and feelings about the issues.

Communication Skills

Improvisation

Divide the class into **A**s and **B**s. Call the **A**s together and give them instruction cards relating to three conversations they are going to have with their **B** partner. Tell them not to let the **B**s see them.

A Instructions

Spend 2–3 minutes in conversation with **B** on each of the given topics. At the end of each conversation discuss what was happening and how it made you feel.

Conversation 1: Share something which is important to you with B.
Conversation 2: Try to find something out about B.
Conversation 3: Talk about a personal worry or problem with B.

Call the **B**s together and give them instruction cards relating to three conversations they are going to have with their **A** partner. Tell them not to let the **A**s see them.

B Instructions

A will engage you in conversation for 2–3 minutes on three given topics. You should respond as indicated below. At the end of each conversation discuss what was happening and how it made you feel.

Conversation 1: Listen but avoid any eye contact with **A** and do nothing that shows any interest.
Conversation 2: Respond to **A** but don't give anything away about yourself.
Conversation 3: Ignore what **A** is saying but talk about yourself

---

Group feedback. Suggest some 'golden rules' about talking to others and listening to others based on the experience of the improvisations.

Listen and follow

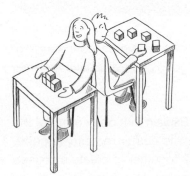

Pupils sit in pairs opposite one another divided by a screen, or back to back. Each pupil has a set of building blocks (Lego, Duplo or similar). Partner **A** creates a shape (the level of complexity will vary with the age of the pupils). Partner **B** has to recreate this exactly by following the verbal instructions of **A** but without having seen what **A** has created. Partners swap roles and repeat the exercise. This helps to develop communication and listening skills. A variation would be to provide pictures or drawings of shapes instead of blocks.

Follow-up discussion should focus on: What difficulties did they have? Were there any misunderstandings? What caused them? In what ways is this like communicating in ordinary life?

Conflict

You need newspaper or magazine articles describing six real-life conflict situations. Get six people to read these out, asking the group to visualise what it is like for the real people in these situations. Divide pupils into six groups, each group taking one of the conflict scenarios. Analyse the problem using the following questions:

- What is the problem?
- Who is affected?
- Where does it happen?
- Why does it happen?
- How could it be tackled?
- What is the best way forward?
- Who will take action?

Follow-up discussion should focus on: Which of the above questions is the most difficult to answer? Why? Can you find any causes of conflict that are common to all the situations? Have you experienced any of these causes of conflict in your own life? Who has to take action?

Variation
Use newspaper or magazine articles which relate to other areas of human experience such as reconciliation, anger, heroism.

Continuum

Use of a continuum can allow pupils to express their thoughts anonymously and give great scope for group and class discussions.

Numbers 1–10 are written on A4 paper and placed in a line on the floor or on the wall (space is needed for pupils to stand by the numbers). 1 means **strongly agree** and 10 means **strongly disagree**. Pupils are given a continuum statement sheet containing the statements you are going to be exploring with 1–10 under each statement. Pupils must not look at it until everyone in the room has one and is ready to start. Everybody must use a pencil so an individual cannot be identified by the colour of their pen. Pupils mark the number (by any agreed method – tick, cross, circle) which most closely reflects their opinion for each statement. There should be no consultation with other members of the group. Each sheet is then folded in half and everyone passes their paper to someone else in the group, who then passes it to someone else, repeating this five times so that it is not possible to identify whose paper is with whom. The leader of the session should read out the statements one at a time. Pupils then go to stand in a line by the number placed on the floor or on the wall which represents the ringed number on the sheet they have been given, thus creating a human bar chart!

Variation

A role-play variation of this is to then ask individuals to speak on behalf of the view they are representing. Asking individuals from widely different points of view generates some interesting discussions and encourages pupils to think about points of view other than their own.

An example of a continuum worksheet is shown below. It may be relevant in some cases to know whether the respondent is male or female since there could be marked divisions between the sexes on some issues. This will not show up on the human bar chart, however, as a boy may be representing a girl's response and vice versa. If it is considered important, male and female responses could be distinguished by pupils wearing different coloured paper hats.

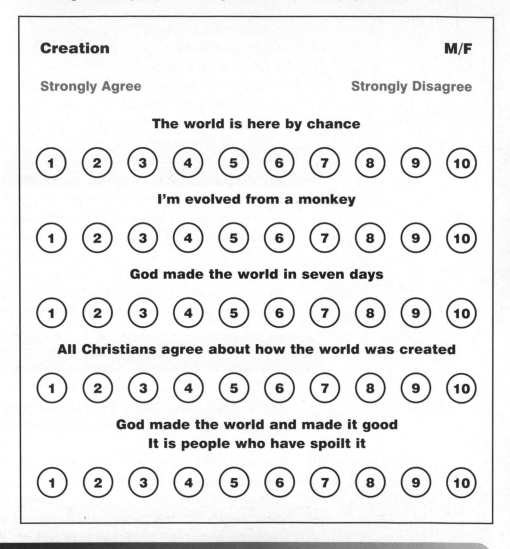

Creation   **M/F**

Strongly Agree   Strongly Disagree

The world is here by chance

① ② ③ ④ ⑤ ⑥ ⑦ ⑧ ⑨ ⑩

I'm evolved from a monkey

① ② ③ ④ ⑤ ⑥ ⑦ ⑧ ⑨ ⑩

God made the world in seven days

① ② ③ ④ ⑤ ⑥ ⑦ ⑧ ⑨ ⑩

All Christians agree about how the world was created

① ② ③ ④ ⑤ ⑥ ⑦ ⑧ ⑨ ⑩

God made the world and made it good
It is people who have spoilt it

① ② ③ ④ ⑤ ⑥ ⑦ ⑧ ⑨ ⑩

Dance and Movement

As an alternative to drama or mime, dance can be used to express spiritual or religious concepts, for example hope, forgiveness, love, compassion.

Debate

Pupils prepare a speech to argue for or against a motion, and others prepare short speeches 'from the floor' to lend support to one side. The speech is timed

(5–6 minutes) and those from the floor should be no more than 2 minutes. At the end of the debate a vote is taken and the motion 'carried' or 'defeated'.

Note
- The motion needs to be carefully worded.
- Pupils need adequate time and support in preparing their speeches – it can be useful to enroll the help of colleagues in other curriculum areas.
- You need to have a 'fall back' position worked out in case key participants are absent on the day, for example understudies prepared to stand in, key points for discussion ready.

Possible motions
- This house believes that money is the root of all evil.
- This house believes that prayer is answered.
- This house believes that abortion is wrong in all circumstances.

These are merely representative of a wide range of issues that could be debated. Ideally individuals should be given an opportunity to express their own considered opinion following the debate.

Diary Entry

This empathetic exercise helps pupils to reflect on the feelings and experiences of characters within biblical (or other) stories. Careful follow-up activities enable pupils to reflect on such feelings in their own lives.

Singly or in pairs, pupils write pages of a diary for the different characters of a well known story, for example The Two Sons (The Bible, Luke 15:11–32).

- The father – on the day his son left home.
- The friend – on the day the money ran out.
- The pig farmer – on the day the son asked for a job.
- The son – on the day he returned home.
- The brother – on the day his brother returned home.
- And what about the missing mother?

When completed the pages are read out to the group.

Diary of Reflection

Diaries of reflection provide pupils with opportunities for quiet, structured reflection on issues of spiritual and moral worth or concern. Many young people will be used to keeping diaries and writing confidential notes to friends. Here a similar means of self-expression is built into lesson activities. Usually the time spent on diary writing will be brief; often pupils are asked to complete a series of unfinished statements. The decision to share these inner thoughts and feelings is left to the pupil. Some will be happy to share ideas and often these stimulate thoughtful discussion. Basic ground rules need to be established at the start and confidentiality must be respected by all if pupils are to gain maximum benefit. The teacher provides the opportunity and creates the appropriate atmosphere.

Basic ground-rules

- Diaries of reflection are most effective when pupils are given regular opportunities to complete them in a quiet disciplined exercise in an atmosphere of reflection.
- Unfinished statements are written on the board and used as a starting point. As pupils get more experienced with this activity, encourage them to suggest the starting points ... but always have some suggestions of your own ready.
- Confidentiality must be respected. No pupils' reflections must be read out or seen by other pupils, or teachers other than the class teacher, without the pupil's permission.
- Pupils should know that their diaries are valued and stored securely by the teacher.
- From time to time the teacher should write a positive, encouraging or questioning comment in response to one of the pupil's reflections.

When introducing Diaries of Reflection for the first time it may be helpful to say something along the following lines.

Your Diary of Reflection is an opportunity to stop your busy life for a few moments and think deeply about your own thoughts, feelings and beliefs. These moments will help you discover the most important directions and values in your life. They will help you to build a picture of the things that really matter to you and the kind of person you are becoming. Use them well and allow others to do the same.

(Based on Michael Beesley, *Space for the Spirit*, Salisbury Diocesan Board of Education)

Discussion Groups

The key to success lies with careful planning in terms of group size, seating arrangements and strategies for ensuring pupil co-operation and participation. Teachers need to be clear about what they want the pupils to achieve through working in the discussion groups (clear learning objectives) and to have thought carefully about how group size, seating arrangements and strategies are going to help to achieve the set learning objectives.

Group size

What is the most effective group size going to be to achieve what you want to achieve? How skilled is the class at participating in group discussion? What are their strengths and weaknesses? How can you encourage them to build on their strengths and overcome their weaknesses?

Begin with discussion in pairs and move on to threes or fours.

As pupils have mastered skills for small group discussion move to groups of 5–6. Larger groups require higher skills and more co-operation.

Seating arrangements

Pairs
This can be a useful way of encouraging a more reserved pupil to share thoughts and feelings. It can be a first step to group discussion.

Trios
This arrangement is useful when an observer or recorder is required. The roles should be rotated.

Small groups
These can either be self-selected or selected randomly (or by some other criterion) by the teacher.

Whole class
This provides a wider audience but can lead to less active participation from some. Are the seating arrangements suitable for class discussion to take place?

Circle within a circle
This is a development from paired discussion. Pupils form an inner circle facing out opposite to a circle of pupils facing in. Pupils discuss their opinion with the partner opposite and then one circle moves round one place to bring everyone face to face with a new partner. This provides one-to-one discussion but with many different partners. It is confidence building for the less self-assured and is clearly structured, providing support for learning.

Circle
This allows everyone, including the teacher, to be an equal partner in the discussion. It encourages pupils to take the lead and everyone to discuss on an equal basis.

Strategies

The following are some strategies designed to get everyone involved:

Brainstorming
See separate entry for this.

Snowballing
A variation on brainstorming. Pupils are presented with a question, dilemma or issue for discussion. Each pupil shares his or her thoughts with a partner. The pair combine with another pair, agree a group opinion or plan of action and either appoint a spokesperson to give a brief report back to the class as a whole, or use the plan of action to complete the task.

'I think' or 'I believe'
A strategy which gives pupils opportunities to question their own opinions or standpoints on a particular question or range of questions relating to a specific issue. The learning strategy also gives pupils the opportunity to question the beliefs of others and justify their own beliefs. Place the class in groups of four or five. Give each pupil a blank card and ask them to write their name clearly on it. Each group is given a bank of statements on a given topic and three other

cards (Agree, Disagree, Not Sure). Each person is then asked to place their name card on the card which reflects their opinion. They could do this before the group briefly discusses the statement or afterwards. Encourage members to look for similarities and differences in opinion within the group and question each other's points of view.

Continuum

See separate entry. As described under the separate entry, the activity is for a whole class and is designed to afford pupils anonimity. It can be modified for use with smaller groups with individual opinions identified. For example, each pupil in a group of six could fill in a continuum worksheet privately before discussion begins. The group then has to reach a consensus based on the individual opinions expressed. This ensures that every individual's starting position is examined in the ensuing discussion.

Interviewing

Divide the class into two, interviewers and interviewees. As a preparation homework interviewers could think of questions they need to ask and intervie-wees could think about the issue and their opinion on it. An interviewer is paired with an interviewee – asks their questions, gets the responses, making a brief record (tape recording could be used). Repeat up to five times. The interviewers then spend some time going through the responses and synthesising the information to get a general feeling about the opinions of the interviewees (possibly for homework). The interviewees meanwhile join together in twos or threes to discuss their opinions – similarities, differences. Interviewers report back to the rest of the class. For the next issue, reverse the roles.

Pass the orange

Pupils sit in a circle. One person is given a large orange (or similar item). A discussion starter is read out. Only the person with the orange can comment. Everyone must give the person speaking their full attention. When he or she has finished the orange is passed to the next person in the circle, who may comment on the original statement or a previous speaker's observations on it. (Ground-rules may need to be established on appropriate forms of expression, particularly when expressing disagreement, for example 'Against what **X** said, I think … ' rather than '**X** was talking a load of rubbish'!) When using this for the first time select non-threatening topics for discussion such as 'watching television'. As the class gains confidence topics can become more 'personal'. Do not intervene too much and be patient with pupils who find it difficult. Regular use of this activity will encourage partici-pation and openness.

Statement response

A story or article is read which raises issues or reveals attitudes to be discussed within the lesson. In response to a specific question, for example, 'Is it always wrong to take human life?' pupils write their views on slips of paper which are then collected in and read out. This allows pupils to contribute anonymously and encourages thoughtful, personal opinions to be expressed in writing.

Can of worms

Discussion questions on a particular theme (either devised by the pupils or the teacher) are written on slips of paper, cut up and placed in a jar. The jar is

passed around the group, each person taking a question out and responding to it. Sentence completion is useful for this activity, for example:

- 'I feel (angry) when ... '
- 'My idea of heaven is ... '
- 'My hope for the world is ... '

When using this with 'a circle within a circle', pupils on the inside pick out a question each, the outer circle rotates, the pupil asks the same question to each partner, noting down opinions for later feedback to the group as a whole. Outer and inner circles swap roles half way through the activity.

Drama

Sacred literature as drama
Sacred writings contain some of the richest dramatic texts and their stories are often acted out in dance and drama during festivals. Some examples are:

- The story of the Nativity – Christmas, Christianity
- The story of the Exodus – Passover, Judaism
- The story of Esther – Purim, Judaism
- The story of Rama and Sita – Diwali, Hinduism

Dramatisation of parables, sayings and stories into a modern idiom enables pupils to explore and express their understanding of the meaning of the text for today.

Ritual as sacred drama
Within religious worship there are rituals which form sacred drama, for example the communion service in Christianity and the seder meal in Judaism. Whilst these are open to study and representation, care must be taken not to trivialise them. As in any dramatic activity, pupils must be encouraged to think themselves into the part – in this case, that of the reverent worshipper within the faith community. This is not encouraging children to worship, but to behave *as if they were worshippers* for the purpose of getting inside a faith.

E   Email from ...

This simple idea can be used in many ways. You can ask pupils to write email from the past, from the future, from the angels, from heaven or hell, from a particular country or situation or in a particular ethical dilemma.

The conventions of email are quite informal, the register of writing often brief, to the point, sometimes witty. If you can, use the school's ICT facilities to do this for real, but if you can't get into the computer room, then the activity can still work.

An example email from the past
At the end of a unit of work on the last week of Jesus' life, pupils in pairs randomly draw a character from a list of all those in the story. Characters

could include the donkey's owner, a market trader from the temple, Pilate's wife, a soldier from the guard on the tomb, as well as the more obvious leading players such as Judas, Mary, Nicodemus, Peter, Caiaphas or Simon of Cyrene. Pupils are asked to study their part of the story carefully, and write a short email message, describing and explaining what they know. The teacher can then get pairs of pupils to swap the messages, and answer each other. The activity opens up dialogue and draws attention to contrasting perspectives, as well as giving pupils a chance to read and think about each other's work.

Freeze Frame

Set up a scene as if it were a video freeze frame or a still from a play. One approach is to ask pupils to mime the action of a story (for example, the Good Samaritan from the Bible, Luke 10:25–37), warning them that you are going to call out 'freeze frame' as they perform their mime. They must then freeze and you will go round and touch different characters on the shoulder. They then have to share their thoughts and feelings (in role) with the rest of the group. You can move the story on by calling 'action' and stopping it again by calling 'freeze frame' and repeating the process. The activity encourages pupils to explore in role the feelings and experiences of those in the story. A follow-up activity is to ask pupils to reflect on times in their own lives when they may have experienced similar feelings.

Games

The following general games may be adapted for different classroom purposes.

Give us a clue
You produce a mystery object and ask them what they think it is. The pupils take it in turns to ask for clues. You may have to help them with other clues later on. A variation is to give an individual something to convey to the group using non-verbal language, for example a feeling, a situation, a person.

Mystery words
A fun way of introducing new words, based on a TV programme. For each word offer two or three descriptions, only one of which is true. This can be done by splitting the group into two teams. Each group has two or three new words and right and wrong answers. After group **A** reads out the word and the possible answers group **B** has to decide which is the right definition. (Variation on *Call My Bluff* TV programme)

Simon says ...
Based on the activity song 'Simple Simon says put your hand on your head, foot, nose' and so on. Go through several times and then add 'yourself' or 'the bit of you which is "I"'. This is useful as a discussion starter on, 'What makes me, me?' or 'Who am I?' Suitable for younger pupils but older pupils enjoy it as well!

Just a minute

Useful as a means of getting pupils talking at the start of a new topic or to draw together learning at the end of a topic. This is based on the long-running radio programme. Pupils have to speak for a minute on a given topic (for example, money, the causes of suffering, what matters most in life, life after death, good and evil) without hesitation, deviation or repetition. Points are awarded to the challenger for a correct challenge and the challenger takes over the speaking. Points are awarded to the speaker for an incorrect challenge and for being the one who is speaking when the 60 seconds is up. An extra point is given to the speaker if they complete the 60 seconds without being successfully interrupted.

Designing a board game

Using the basic idea of a simple board game such as snakes and ladders, pupils design a game on an RE theme, for example 'Journey of Life'.

Who are you?

After completing a unit of work on religious leaders, have a picture of one religious leader on an OHT, covered with a piece of paper cut into jig-saw type pieces. Pupils are divided into teams of four. Each team in turn is asked a question from the course. A section of the picture is uncovered for each correct answer and the team given the chance to identify the person. The team which correctly identifies the person wins. The game can be extended by continuing with another religious leader and totalling up the number of correct identifications each team has made at the end. This technique could be used at the end of other topics or units, for example places of worship, Islam, religious artefacts with an appropriate selection of pictures being used.

Gift for Life

Give everyone two sheets of paper. Ask them to write down in the middle of one the word 'Gift'. Brainstorm everything which comes to mind. Ask the pupils to cross out any words which are things money can buy. Ask them to focus on 'gifts' which money cannot buy – spend one or two minutes in quiet reflection. Now using the other sheet of paper, ask pupils to write down, and illustrate if they want, something they would like to give the person on their left to 'help them on their journey of life'. Allow a few minutes and then ask everyone to pass on their gifts.

Feedback: What have people been given? What are their thoughts about their gift?

Variation

Have a series of photographs of people in different situations (for example, someone very rich, poor, tired, hungry, happy, bereaved). Complete as above until the moment of quiet reflection, then use the photographs and in pairs or trios write down and illustrate, if they want to, the gifts they would offer that person.

Follow up: Explore 'the gift' which God offers to believers, for example Jesus; gifts of the Spirit; Allah, the giver of life and health.

Guided Visualisation

This involves the teacher guiding the pupils through an imaginative visualisation. After a period of 'stilling', the teacher begins to construct a scene and slowly guides the pupils though it. The aim is to engage the imagination and feelings. An essential aspect is the debriefing period immediately following the exercise, during which the teacher provides opportunities for participants to explore how they felt and what they experienced. Activities follow which allow pupils to express and develop their insights. Scripting biblical stories as guided visualisations is a good way of engaging pupils imaginatively with the events of the story.

Scripts for guided visualisations are to be found in many sources including *Don't Just Do Something, Sit There*, Mary Stone, RMEP and *New Methods in R.E. Teaching: An Experiential Approach*, John Hammond and David Hay (eds), Oliver & Boyd.

Some guidelines

Before

- When using guided visualisation for the first time with a group, ask for co-operation and invite them to share responsibility for what happens. Start small – don't expect them to be able to participate in a 40-minute guided visualisation straight away.
- Seek to create the right atmosphere. Think about the positioning of furniture. Should the participants sit in a circle? Do the blinds need drawing? Should you have music playing in the background? Would a lighted candle provide a useful focal point?
- Have an alternative activity ready in case things don't go to plan.
- Think about how you can best help participants to feel secure and comfortable – tell them that if at any time they start to feel uncomfortable they can open their eyes and stop taking part (whilst not stopping others from doing so of course).
- Negotiate ground-rules for the group.
- Minimise the risk of interruption – put a note on the outside of the classroom door asking not to be disturbed.

During

- Start in a clear reassuring way. Be confident, speak firmly, be in charge of the activity, tell the pupils what to do.
- Allow for 'opt out', 'none-active participation', 'the observer role' but without disturbing others (fundamental ground-rule).
- Begin with a stilling exercise – sit up, both feet on the floor, hands together on the lap or one hand on each knee, breathing (normal at first, then a little slower and deeper), listening (to sounds outside room, inside room, of person breathing who is next to you, your own breathing), relaxing, practising self-awareness.
- Speak calmly and don't forget to allow appropriate pauses in the narrative.
- Keep an eye on the time – allow plenty of time for debriefing and follow-up.

- Finish by inviting them 'when you are ready' to 'open your eyes … ', stretch (sensibly – ground-rule) and relax.
- Do not allow talking immediately (ground-rule) – have a short pause in silence.

After

The follow-up activity or activities should be given about the same amount of time as the guided visualisation. Activities could include:
- creative art work (drawing, painting);
- writing (poetry, diary of reflection, summary note);
- drama (role-play, mime, freeze frame, dance);
- discussion (paired, small group, whole class) – pupils should be free to share their experience of the guided visualisation or not (ground-rule).

Follow-up discussion (paired, small group or whole class) must ensure that:
- pupils are given adequate time to share ideas, thoughts and feelings;
- pupils are encouraged to listen carefully and sensitively to the ideas, thoughts and feelings of others;
- pupils are helped to articulate their learning through the experience.

H   Hot Seat

One member of the group sits centrally and can be asked any question from the floor which they answer from the perspective of a specified role. Teachers and other adults can be in the Hot Seat, answering in role or for themselves. Pupils should *not* be required to answer for themselves.

Examples of use

Visitor
In the hot seat 'for real'. Pupils prepare questions in advance.

Pupil in role
This can be used to consolidate a unit of work exploring the life and work of an individual, for example Martin Luther King, Mahatma Gandhi. This requires careful preparation – pupils may submit questions to the person in the hot seat (and his or her group of advisors) in advance so that they may do some research. Pupils' questions must arise from their own research.

Beat the teacher
Pupils are asked to research and prepare questions to ask the teacher. They may work individually or in teams. When asking factual questions pupils must know the answers to the questions. Teams may compete to see which is able to 'beat the teacher'.

I   Ice Breakers

These are short activities designed to break down barriers, introduce people and encourage participation.

Circle games

Fruit salad

The group sits in a circle facing the centre. Each member of the group is designated by the name of a fruit – orange, apple, pear, banana, grape, peach. The person in the centre calls out 'banana' and all the 'bananas' change places, but as the person in the middle has now joined in, there is one person left standing, who in turn calls out another fruit. If the person in the centre calls out 'fruit salad' everyone moves.

Everyone who ...

One person in the centre of the circle shouts out a statement and everyone to whom it applies changes places. Examples: 'Everyone who has a cat,' 'Everyone who loves (or hates) football.'

Name Games

Getting to know you

Everyone takes it in turn to introduce himself or herself by choosing and doing an alliterative action, for example dancing Duncan, sitting Sam. A variation on this activity is for everyone in turn to call out their name, their favourite colour and something they can do (however simple) or something they like. This could be followed up with the next activity.

Name volley

- A bean bag or small cushion is thrown around the circle, each person calling out their own name before throwing it to someone else (2–3 minutes);
- Repeat with each person calling out their own name and the name of the person they are throwing to (2–3 minutes);
- Repeat calling out only the other person's name before they throw.

Name build

The group sits in a circle and person **A** starts by saying their own name. Person **B** then says **A**'s name followed by their own. Person **C** says **A**'s name, **B**'s name and their own. And so on ...

Name likes

This continues on from name building. Person **A** starts again and adds something that they like, for example 'My name is Mike and I like athletics.' It continues as above.

Who am I?

Everyone sits in a circle. The teacher calls out categories of people, for example people who play sport; people who play a musical instrument; people who don't like *Neighbours* and so on. Anyone belonging to the category goes and sits in the middle of the circle. If they belong to the next category they stay in; otherwise they return to their seats.

Acrostics

Pupils write their names down a sheet of A4 paper in large letters and use each letter of their name as the first letter of a word which describes some personal characteristic. Seated in a circle, pupils then read out their acrostics and tell the rest of the group something about themselves.

I Am
Each member of the group is given a piece of card and asked to write down any six things about themselves – but they must not be physically descriptive statements. When everyone is finished all the cards are collected in, shuffled and redistributed. As they are read out the group tries to work out who is who.

Picture Me

Each member of the group is asked to draw a picture to present to the rest of the group that says something about them. Again they are presented anonymously and the group try to work out who they belong to.

Interviews

Interviewing a visitor or conducting a series of interviews to gather facts or opinions from a variety of people can be a worthwhile experience for pupils in trying to assimilate information and synthesise ideas. Interviews can be conducted in role (as a newspaper reporter or radio journalist).

Note
The success of this kind of exercise depends crucially on the interviewer having researched the topic thoroughly and developed appropriate questions which will elicit the required information. A key question which all interviewers should be clear about is what it is they are trying to find out.

In the News

Pupils are asked to bring in newspaper cuttings which illustrate how beliefs affect actions in today's world. These will be both positive and negative. Examples may include such things as: terrorist bombings, expressing the belief of a minority that human life can be sacrificed to bring about political power; a person giving a kidney to save the life of another, expressing the belief in altruism and caring for others. Ask pupils to decide what belief is behind the action. Make a wall display entitled 'Belief in Action'.

Development
Explore with pupils the ways in which religious beliefs have influenced the way people, both in the past and present, live their lives, for example St Francis of Assisi, the Prophet Muhammad (peace be upon him), Mahatma Gandhi, Mother Teresa of Calcutta.

Invite a visitor into school to talk with or be interviewed by the pupils about how their faith affects the way they live.

Jigsaw

A piece of text is cut up into a number of pieces, muddled and given out to a group. Pupils read out each section and decide together the correct order of the pieces. These are then stuck onto a sheet of paper. This encourages co-operative working and engages pupils with the text so that they have to discern its meaning.

Kaleidoscope

This optical instrument contains two to four reflecting surfaces placed in a tube, at one end of which is a container holding coloured glass. Looking into the kaleidoscope a person sees a rainbow of brightly coloured symmetrical patterns that can be changed by turning the end of the tube.

In groups pupils take it in turn to look into a kaleidoscope and explain what they see. Exploring pattern and symmetry as an introduction to looking at issues of beauty and diversity in nature leads on to discussion about how, or by whom, that beauty and diversity was 'created' and is sustained.

Pupils can be asked to look for pattern and symmetry in nature – what do they see in the clouds, rain falling on a window pane, when they look at a tree, or the pattern seen from the back of a leaf. They may paint a picture showing pattern and symmetry in nature.

Kitchen

Food plays an important role in religion. Dietary laws reflect, for example, beliefs about creation and about humanity's relationship with the created world, with each other and with God.

Take the opportunity to cook some food which would traditionally be eaten by members of a particular religion during one of their festivals (for example, hot cross buns for Christians at Easter, latkes for Jews at Hanukkah). Talk about their significance and think about their symbolism.

Make a class or school cook book including favourite recipes from a range of religions. This could then be sold as a fundraising exercise and the proceeds given to a charity which is seeking to alleviate hunger in the world.

Knapsack

A knapsack is a bag which is strapped to the back to carry a soldier's necessities. A popular song in Britain from the early years of the 20th century goes:

'I love to go a-wandering, along the mountain track;
and as I go I love to sing, my knapsack on my back.'

Today we might call it a rucksack.

Imagine that you are going on a long journey (to somewhere hot or cold, isolated or busy for example). All you can take with you are the things that you can fit into your knapsack – the bare necessities. What would you choose to take and why? Now imagine that you can put not only things but qualities into your knapsack (kindness, friendship and so on). On your journey through life what qualities are you, or would you like to be, taking with you?

(The CEM publication *Looking Inwards – Looking Outwards* has a story and activities which develop this further. *See* student's book page 22 and activity sheets 6 and 7)

Listening

Listening skills are really crucial in RE, where pupils often have to try and understand something which seems distant, strange or new to them. Listening skills also matter for classroom dialogue: children and adults can both fall victim to the easy idea that 'I hear what you're saying' when actually the other person's viewpoint is hardly heard at all.

Here are three simple strategies to encourage more active listening, which can be related to a variety of RE discussion topics, from 'Why do they do that?' – discussions of photographs of worship distributed among six year olds – to structured debates about the sanctity of life with sixteen year olds.

Back to back

Sit pupils in pairs back to back, and ask one to describe, and the other to draw an object, artefact or picture. This focuses sharply on the listening skills of the person drawing the picture, and requires a very active ear. Or use this strategy to simulate a telephone conversation, for instance for older pupils someone phoning a helpline with a particular moral dilemma to consider. The role of 'telephone counsellor', well done, is one of the most active listening roles in the world!

Hearing and listening: 'I will say this only once'

Put pupils in small groups, and get one to lead by reading a passage, or telling a story. After listening to the talker, pupils are asked a number of questions about what they heard to check out their listening, or they are asked to reconstruct as much as they can of what was said. This gives instant feedback about who was listening, and who was only hearing.

Good and bad listeners

With pupils, make a list of characteristics of good listeners and bad listeners. The list might be something like the one shown on the next page. Get pupils to choose a topic, and role-play being good and bad listeners in threes: one talks, one is a good listener, the other a bad listener. Use this in reviewing work or revising, as a study skill builder.

Good	Bad
Looks you in the eye	Attention wanders
Is interested in you	Seems bored
Nods to show they've heard you	Keeps interrupting
Smiles	Looks away
Asks questions	Tells you what they think but never asks what you think

Mental Maps

This strategy provides an opportunity for pupils to express, communicate, and reflect on their mental images of the world and of world issues. Pupils are asked to imagine a situation or scene, for example the following.

A Martian lands from outer space. You are the first human it meets. It is friendly and intelligent but doesn't speak your language. You draw a map of planet earth to show the Martian what is currently going on.

This may be adapted for wider use, for example to draw a mental map representing where pupils are now in relation to their past, their family, their hopes for the future, their ideas for the rest of the world; to express or map out feelings or emotions for a given life circumstance such as divorce, death, moving house or school, broken friendships. (There is need for sensitivity and careful handling and follow up here).

Pupils can make their maps as detailed or as representative as they like, making sure they can 'translate' what they mean to others later if asked. They may like to use lines, squares, full stops, wheels – whatever helps them to think about and express their ideas.

Mime

Pupils, working in pairs or small groups, devise a mime to represent the outward expression of an inner feeling (anger, sympathy) or moral virtue (goodness, generosity, compassion). The process of working out the mime focuses the attention of the pupil and helps to raise awareness of the power of inner feelings.

Music

Music can be used effectively to aid reflection on religious concepts, for example exploring the themes of change and death. You may have talked about Jesus' death, or rites of passage studying death rituals within religion. Listening and responding to music is one way of helping pupils reflect on their own attitudes to death.

Example

Play a part of Grieg's *Springtime* – a reflective piece composed to accompany a poem in which the poet welcomes the new life of spring whilst reflecting that it may be his last. Ask pupils to think of the cycle of life and death and simultaneously doodle shapes and patterns on paper to express ideas and feelings. Pupils then talk about their thoughts and feelings with a partner. Go on to explore religious ideas about life and death, and how pupils view them. Or use modern classics such as Paul Simon's *Leaves That Are Green* or more recent songs. (Do not try to be 'with it' concerning current musical tastes unless you really are. Ask the pupils to name current songs which raise the issues you want to discuss and to bring in their tapes – but listen to them yourself before using them).

News Boards

This activity is a way of encouraging self worth and the valuing of others. It provides a structure for enabling pupils within a group (tutor group or primary school class) to share important personal experiences and encourages each child to be sensitive and appreciative towards the values and feelings of others. Pupils are invited to place on the news board items of personal interest or concern. Discussion around the area or issue raised can take place.

Variation

A news board can be changed into a questions board and pupils encouraged to put on it any questions they have relating to the topic they are studying. Other pupils might like to try to answer them.

News Bulletins

These are useful as a way of consolidating pupil learning from a lesson or series of lessons. Small groups prepare a one-minute radio news bulletin on the lesson topic. The group elects a 'newsreader'. Each bulletin has 60 seconds only, and bulletins follow in quick succession.

Observation

Giving attention is at the heart of spirituality. Developing the ability to 'see' with insight, awareness and appreciation is a key dimension of spiritual development. Providing pupils with opportunities for long, slow looking encourages reflection and helps pupils to 'see' in a different way, developing spiritual awareness. The following examples of activities would fit well into RE lessons exploring creation, 'Who am I?' or human nature.

Example activities

Ask pupils to observe closely their own hands (or face or eyes in a mirror, or a partner's eyes). Compare finger prints, line patterns on the palm of the hand, the shades of colour and shape in different peoples' eyes. Consider how each person is unique and special. Pupils could consider what they like and don't like about themselves, what they can and cannot change, what they're good at, what skills they can do with their hands, how their hands can help others.

Also, close observation of nature such as minibeasts, spiders' webs, plants or tree bark from the school grounds – or frost, icicles, ice or snow.

Talk about:
- what pupils have noticed for the first time;
- what their careful looking made them think about;
- what they felt.

Give pupils the opportunity to record these sights, thoughts and feelings creatively in words or drawings.

P

Paper Chain

Pupils write their own thoughts on small lengths of sticky-backed paper which are then made into loops and joined together to form a chain which is displayed. This activity has many applications.

A prayer chain
Pupils write their own prayers or poems relating to a lesson focus.

A chain of hope
Pupils write their hopes for the world.

The chain of life
As part of a study of the wholeness and interdependence of creation, pupils choose one of the vital elements for human life – for example fire, light, air, water, soil, plants, living creatures (humans and animals) – and express their thoughts about the value of this element. These are then linked together to form a complete circle. Pupils are asked to talk about what happens if one element or one link in the chain is damaged. Who or what might 'break the chain'? Why? How can we prevent this?

Values chain
Pupils write about one key value that they believe is vital for a happy and fulfilled life lived together in community.

Paper and Pen

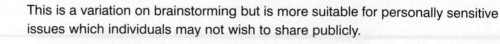

This is a variation on brainstorming but is more suitable for personally sensitive issues which individuals may not wish to share publicly.

Example: My greatest fear
Give out pieces of paper and pens. Ask everyone to write down the headings: This Lesson; School; Life in General. Ask them secretly to write down their greatest fear or worry concerning each. Ask them to fold them up and place them into a container passed around by the teacher. These can then be read out (being careful to ensure anonymity). Commonly held worries and fears will be identified. Pupils go into groups, each group to be given one fear or worry which is shared by many. Groups suggest three things a person with this fear or worry could do.

Photoboard

This is the telling of a story using a sequence of photographs or images taken from magazines with dialogue superimposed in speech bubbles. Pupils are asked to produce a short narrative which raises a moral dilemma. The end result provides a stimulus for discussion of issues and involves other individuals and classes through display. (The CEM publication *Dilemmas and Decisions* offers 48 situations which pose moral dilemmas. These could be used as starting points.)

Photographs and Pictures

Get 'inside' a photograph or picture by 'interrogating' it – asking questions of those in the picture, exploring actions, motives, relationships and so on. For example, when looking at a picture of an event, ask questions like ...

- What can you see in the picture?
- What are the people doing?
- What might they be saying?
- Have you seen anything like this before?
- Can you see all the people who have shared in planning or running this event or are some of them outside the picture?
- What might have been done by some of the people we cannot see?
- What would happen if one person in this group suddenly stopped taking part?
- How do you think each person is feeling? Have you ever felt like that?

The actual questions will naturally vary depending on the subject matter.

Variation

Using Christmas cards with specifically Christian images, cut up and stick pictures on a sheet to form a design. Pupils then write questions around these for others to answer. This activity encourages pupils to look carefully, analyse, reflect and interpret the meaning and significance of the images on the cards.

Poetry

The reading and writing of poetry exercises the imagination and helps articulate ideas and feelings which cannot easily be expressed in any other way. A poem was once described as 'an ice-axe to break open the ice-block of our soul'. The following simple structures can be used to encourage pupils to write down their inner thoughts and feelings.

Cinquaines

These are five-line poems which have the following structure.

1 word	PEACE
2 words	BRINGS HARMONY
3 words	MAKES PEOPLE HAPPY
2 words	DEPENDS ON
1 word	US

Septaines

These are seven-line poems in the same form as a cinquaine (that is, 1 word – 2 words – 3 words – 4 words – 3 words – 2 words – 1 word).

Haikus

The haiku is a 3-line poetic form originating in Japan. The traditional form is five *syllables* (not words), followed by seven, followed by five. The poem captures a moment of awareness or insight and should be written spontaneously to capture the essence of the experience.

> Those who close their minds
> To wonder and delight are
> Blinder than the blind

Sonnets

For older pupils (especially those studying Shakespeare) try using sonnets. Have a word with your English specialist if you are not sure. Sonnets have 14 lines with 10 syllables per line which should have the rhythm ti-tum ti-tum ti-tum ti-tum ti-tum (that is, with the emphasis on the second, fourth, sixth, eighth and tenth syllables). A number of different rhyming patterns were used by classical poets like Milton and Shakespeare but the simplest to adopt is a-b-a-b, c-d-c-d, e-f-e-f, g-g with the final rhyming couplet delivering a 'punchline'. Encourage upper secondary pupils to reflect on human beliefs, values and qualities, or moral issues such as human rights, using this structure. They will amaze you with what they can do given the opportunity. Here is one example.

How would you feel?

How would you feel if you belonged nowhere,
All of your possessions on your sore back?
You are so lost, your families despair
On a long dusty road fearing attack.
How would you feel not knowing who to trust?
Wondering if someone was watching you.
Who have you told? Perhaps you have been sussed,
Vanishing, gone, taken out of the blue.
How would you feel to look death in the face?
The chair, the injection, your final end -
It faces you, your heart begins to pace,
Shaking, spluttering, body beyond mend.
These descriptions all sound like bitter hell.
For some people it's the story that they tell.

Claire Beresford, aged 15,
Thomas Keble School, Eastcombe, Gloucestershire.

(See also 'Poetry based on the senses' under Senses)

'Post-its'

Use these to record pupils' responses – words or phrases – to a piece of narrative, a story or a video, asking them to put themselves in the place of the person, imagining what the person feels in that situation, for example: telling the story of Ibrahim being tempted by Shaytan to rebel against God; exploring how Muslims express their rejection of evil by stoning the pillars during Hajj. This is useful as a means of exploring the emotions and feelings involved in temptation (see *RE Today*, Summer 1995, page 30). Similar responses may be grouped, pupils sticking their word or phrase in the appropriate section of a large sheet of paper.

'Post-its' can also be a simple way of consolidating learning. Pupils create a simple slogan and an illustration on a 'post-it' to express what they have learned from the lesson or unit of work. These can then be stuck on a large sheet of paper and displayed.

Q Question Box

Each pupil prepares a question on a subject. All the questions are then collected into a box and redistributed to other pupils for them to discover the answer.

Examples
- For 7-year-olds: all the questions that you can think of about what makes a hero, or what puzzles you about life and death.
- For 10-year-olds: questions about why there is suffering, or about what's going on in this video clip with the sound turned down (use a clip of worship, for instance).
- For 13-year-olds: questions about what happens when you die, or any questions you would ask God if you could.
- For 16-year-olds: questions about sex ethics, or what you would ask the devil (if there is one).

R Re-enactment

A known event is re-enacted exactly to try to access its dynamics, relationships, meanings and so on. This approach can usefully draw out empathetic feelings from participants. The better the briefing, the better the results. It is useful for dealing with religious story, but take care to avoid offending some faith traditions by casting God. Skilled questioning after the re-enactment can help pupils draw deeper meaning from the story.

Reflective Activities

For this kind of activity a good working relationship, based on trust and consideration of the needs of others is important. Pupils should be seated comfortably in an atmosphere conducive to reflective thinking, using appropriate lighting,

music, and so on. The leader introduces the contemplative activity through words or visual stimuli. The reflective activity is followed up in one of a number of ways, allowing pupils to express and explore their insights and feelings.

Circle time

A structured time when the class gathers in a circle to speak, listen, share joys and concerns. It is essentially about interaction. Practically, a circle is a good way of organising the group so that all can see and be seen, hear and be heard. Symbolically the circle represents co-operation and unity. It indicates mutual support and collaboration. The teacher seeks to provide a supportive and accepting atmosphere and takes part in all the activities. The teacher is the 'facilitator'. A number of activities and approaches can be used, including icebreakers, discussion starters, sharing views and opinions. Circle time is increasingly being used in many primary and in some secondary schools as part of class or tutor time or as an element in a personal and social education programme.

Reflection circle

This is regarded by some practitioners as an essential element in the conclusion of an activity or session. A simple idea of forming a circle in order to gain feedback and share experiences.

(See also Diary of Reflection)

Role-play

In role-play pupils imagine they are in a situation and behave as they would in the role. Pupils are asked to pretend they are the people concerned. Role-play is useful in a learning situation because it:

- helps pupils analyse a problem – re-enacting an incident can help pupils to draw out the important points and think more carefully about what is actually happening;
- helps build pupils' self-confidence to cope with a range of situations by practising how they should behave;
- helps pupils understand the position and feelings of others involved in the situation.

Role-play arouses interest and active participation, but it must be remembered that it is not an end in itself. It is essential that structured reflection and exploration of issues highlighted in the role-play follow. Important questions to address are:

- What was happening in the role-play?
- How did the pupils feel (in role)?
- What did they feel about each other's actions?
- What did they learn from the role-play?

An alternative way of ending a role-play is for a volunteer from the 'audience' to walk up to the 'actors' and in silence arrange them into a tableau (see Human Sculpture) to represent how he or she understood the interaction which had taken place. The observers then discuss what went on in the role-play. The actors return to their seats and give their views.

Opposite are some examples of role-play situations which can be adapted.

Interviews and interrogations

Roles might include: journalists; detectives; scientists; radio reporters; documentary film crews; jurors; police.

Meetings

Simulation of decision making: parish council meeting; public enquiry; protest meeting; school council; action group.

Telephone helpline

Exploration of personal problems – real or imagined. (Sit pupils back to back to avoid all sight of each other, and see how this influences communication. Excellent for developing listening skills.)

Overheard conversation

Hiding, spying, eavesdropping, drama can explore themes like truth and lies, gossip, secrets and so on. Groups of three can develop overheard conversation.

Witness

Taking the role of a participant in an enquiry or trial, each person explains what they saw, heard and knew. This can be useful for exploring religious experience, for example Guru Nanak's disappearance, Paul's conversion.

Note on organisation

Make sure everyone fully understands the role play scenario and their own role within it. Do this by carefully preparing cards which give a summary of the situation on one side and the individual's role description on the other. Allow time for people to familiarise themselves with these and to think themselves 'into role'.

S | Senses

These exercises encourage pupils to become more aware of their various senses.

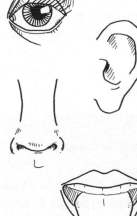

Guess who?

This activity concentrates on the sense of sight (through its absence) and raises awareness of the ability to 'see' through other senses, in this case touch. This can be enacted by a pair or a larger group. It simply involves a blindfolded person recognising another person by touch – as in the TV show *They Think It's All Over* where panelists have to guess the mystery personality by touch alone.

Senses poetry

This exercise can be done using any video clip, poster or picture. Imagine you are a bystander of the scene depicted (or one of the characters in it). Write a six line poem on what you see, hear, taste, smell, touch and feel (one line for each). This basic format can be adapted, for example allocating two lines for each sense or concentrating on only two senses. The format can be as simple or as complex as you require, depending on the ages and aptitudes of the pupils involved. Invite pupils to share their poetry with others. They may be reluctant to voice their poetry, but may be willing for their poem to go into a class book.

Sentence Completion

Many teachers may already use this as a simple means of testing knowledge but its purpose here is different. It is a way of getting pupils to express their own hopes, fears, feelings and self-evaluations. It can be used in a variety of contexts.

In starting discussion (See also 'Can of Worms' under Discussion Groups)
- My idea of heaven is ...
- My hope for the world is ...

For expressing feelings
- I feel (happy) when ...

For reviewing
- I understood ...
- I didn't understand ...

For evaluation
- I enjoyed ...
- I didn't enjoy ...

For observation
- I noticed ...

For negotiation
- I would like to ...

This technique is simple, works well in the classroom, and is an effective way for pupils to tap into their thoughts and feelings. It aids reflective thinking, encourages pupils to clarify their thoughts, feelings and opinions and gives them confidence in expressing them. It promotes listening skills.

The teacher stimulates a discussion by either writing an unfinished sentence for all the class to see (on the board or an OHT) and asks pupils to complete it either verbally or by writing it down before discussing it. Select pupils to share their ideas – for example, ask the back row or table to read out their responses to the first sentence, another group to the second, another to the third and so on – until all pupils have had the opportunity to be involved.

Story

Stories are invaluable tools for spiritual development. They help us to make sense of our own experience and to gain insights from other people's. They explore questions of shared human experience and provide stimulus for the personal search of the individual. Listening to a story may not seem to qualify as an active learning strategy but the point at issue is not whether the pupils are *doing* something but whether they are *engaged*.

The meaning of the teaching-story cannot be unravelled by ordinary intellectual methods alone. Its action is direct and certain, upon the innermost part of the

human being. The closest we can come to describing its effect is to say that it connects with a part of the individual which cannot be easily reached by any other convention ...
Idries Shah, *Caravan of Dreams*

Story grows out of life, reflects it and enters into dialogue with it. All life is in story so that there children will find their experience confirmed, challenged, developed and broadened ...
Maurice Lynch, *Tell Me a Story*

Stories from literature, from faith and secular traditions, and from contemporary society, if selected carefully and explored sensitively, provide important opportunities for personal and spiritual growth in the classroom. Short stories are best, followed by discussion and evaluation or other activities. Stories may be used to introduce a number of the activities described in this book, for example a role-play to continue the story and answer the question, 'What happened next?'

Note on using story from faith traditions

Remember that many of these stories are from the sacred writings of the faith community involved and as such convey religious and spiritual truths to believers and consequently are often revered. In religious education we are seeking to explore the meaning a story holds for believers and to open up the possibility that it connects with the lives of all pupils, irrespective of their faith or non-faith position.

T Trust Games

All of the following need careful preparation and a safe environment (for example, soft mats for landing). The aim is to develop co-operation and confidence in others.

Sitting circle

A group of people (ten or more) form a circle and then sit down. If it is done correctly then everyone is supported by everyone else.

Back to back

In pairs **A** and **B** stand back to back and link through each others arms. They now have to sit down and stand up together.

Feet pull

In pairs **A** and **B** sit facing each other with the soles of their feet touching. Then holding each other's wrists they stand up by pulling.

Blindfold find

All the members of the group are blindfolded and put in different parts of the room. They have to link up with each other as quickly as possible. This is made more difficult if a no talking rule is imposed.

These activities are useful for developing trust and collaboration within the group – essential ingredients to learning in RE, where a 'safe environment' for sharing personal thoughts, beliefs and ideas is necessary.

Prepare strips of coloured paper representing (as nearly as possible) the colours of the rainbow. The seven colours represent different areas of human experience as follows:

Red	Life
Orange	Death
Yellow	Humanity
Green	The World
Blue	Good
Indigo	Evil
Violet	God

There is nothing sacrosanct about these seven categories if you can think of others which might work better with your pupils.

Ask them to think of as many questions as they can under these headings which no one can answer, and to write them on the appropriate coloured strip. If a pupil can think of four questions under one heading and none under another this does not matter. Mix up all the strips in a container so that questions are not attributable to individuals and then sort them into their colours. Make seven groups, one for each colour, and get them to sift the questions (some of which will be the same, or nearly the same) and reduce them to the seven which they think are most interesting or most important. Again there is nothing magical about the number seven. The point is to reduce the questions to a manageable number for display while ensuring that these include the questions the pupils think are most important. These are then used to create a 'rainbow' of ultimate questions.

Various further exercises can then stem from this. Pupils could work in groups to agree which five out of all the questions they would want to ask God to answer if they could. They could then research what 'answers' members of different faiths might suggest. Finally, as a piece of individual work, they could be asked to select the question they find most interesting and important, explaining why they think it interesting and important, and writing everything they can about it without actually answering it.

This exercise is a very powerful way of making pupils think about the difference between scientific or empirical questions and religious questions, and showing that there are areas of human questioning which science cannot touch.

Values

These are various activities which can be employed to help pupils clarify the values which they hold within themselves. (See also Balloon Debate)

Value statements
Make a controversial statement to the whole group and ask them how they feel about it. Define four areas of the room as strongly agree, agree, disagree and

strongly disagree, and ask them to move to the area that best describes how they feel. They can then discuss their thoughts and feelings with the people in their area and then with the full group. You may also want to offer information to the group as a whole. They may decide to move to different positions after their discussions, which is fine. However, the aim is not to change their position but to help them clarify it.

Select a statement
Similar to the above except that you place several statements around the room for the group to choose from. Ask them to go and stand next to the statement that they agree with the most. Continue as above.

Personal statement
Give every group member four cards and ask them to write down a statement on each card on a particular issue. When this has been completed the cards are collected in, shuffled, and then two cards are dealt out to each member. If an individual is satisfied with the statements on the cards they can be kept. If not one card may be exchanged at a time by selecting a new one and throwing the old one away face up. As it moves around the group and comes back it can be chosen again and this way the game continues until the person is satisfied with the cards they have. When this is all complete each member must explain and justify the cards kept. This may be done in small groups or as a whole group.

Visitors

Carefully selected and briefed visitors are an invaluable way to stimulate interest and pupil participation. To generate the right atmosphere and to make the best use of the person's time, both the visitor and the group need to be carefully prepared.

The visitor needs to:
- understand the context of the visit and the amount of time available;
- be told the age and ability of the pupils and the topic they are working on;
- be aware of any important background information he or she needs, especially if dealing with personally sensitive issues;
- discuss with you how they wish to use the session;
- be advised about what to expect in terms of pupil response and participation.

The pupils need to be:
- told who is coming in, when and why;
- briefed on the issues which are to be addressed;
- asked to prepare questions to ask the visitor.

Visitors can be used in the following ways:
- with small groups of pupils, who have the responsibility for preparing an agenda and then the opportunity to practise social skills and learn about the chosen topic;
- with the whole class;
- in a *Question Time* format as a visiting expert prepared to answer questions from the audience.

Visitor preparation activity

This should focus on developing skills of understanding the importance of generating and posing open-ended questions which give the visitor 'space' to explain his or her views; understanding the need for careful listening to hear what the speaker is really saying, not what you expected them to say; sensitivity to appropriate and inappropriate questions, empathising with the visitor's feelings; the courtesies of meeting, greeting, introducing, thanking.

1 Explain the proposed lesson: interviewing a visitor (for example, youth leader, minister, counsellor, imam).
2 Stress the importance of asking questions and listening to answers.
3 Ask pupils to think about whether their questions are 'open' or 'loaded' and whether they could be offensive.
4 Now get groups of four pupils to generate four sensible questions to put to the visitor.

The teacher must discuss: appropriate questions and ground-rules for good behaviour, privacy, open and closed questions. Two or three pupils will be elected or chosen by the teacher to meet, greet, and introduce the visitor. Pupils are also appointed to give a vote of thanks and accompany visitor to reception. These pupils need to rehearse these functions and jobs.

Wall Display

Although not actually an active learning strategy, a wall display of one form or another can be one of the 'by-products' of many of the activities outlined in this publication. Working individually or together to produce something for display provides opportunities to consolidate and extend learning, builds self confidence and increases co-operation. Ann Krisman, working with special needs children, has developed a 'Wall of Wisdom' displaying comments made by pupils in writing or in discussion which show particular insight. For details see *RE Today*, Summer 1999, page 6.

X-Files

In pairs pupils role-play the parts of two 'federal agents', one a believer and the other sceptical about a reported happening, for example one of the miracles of Jesus – the stilling of the storm or the raising of Lazarus. They 'interrogate' their evidence in role.

Yardstick

Pupils are given a statement to act as a 'yardstick' – something to measure everything else by. Examples of yardsticks could be: you should always tell your teacher if someone does something wrong; taking the life of another human being is always wrong.

They are then given, or devise themselves, situations in which that yardstick has to be applied. For example, with regard to telling the teacher when someone has done wrong, the pupil who has done something wrong is (a) someone you don't like (b) your best friend (c) you. Or with regard to the rule that it is always wrong to take life, you are (a) in the army and being sent to fight in a war (b) a doctor deciding whether or not to allow an abortion to a rape victim (c) a man (woman) whose wife (husband) is being threatened by an armed robber.

This is a useful way of stimulating discussion on a particular moral principle or on the wider issue of whether there are moral absolutes and, if not, on what principles you might decide in individual cases.

Yes or No

Devise a list of questions about a particular topic or belief to which the answer is either Yes or No, either right or wrong, either true or false. This could be done as a summary test at the end of a unit of work to assess factual knowledge and simple understanding. (See also Zebra)

Variation
In groups of three or four pupils devise their own questions on an aspect of a given topic or belief which require answers of either Yes or No. They then 'test' another group in the class, who in turn test them on a different aspect. For example, on the theme of the Sikh celebration of Baisakhi, groups in the class are given the aspects: the founding of the Khalsa, the life of Guru Gobind Singh, the Amrit ceremony, and how Baisakhi is celebrated today.

Yo-Yo

This activity is a way of encouraging paired or small group discussion. (See also Discussion Groups)

One person, **A**, starts off the discussion by making a brief statement, which the next person, **B**, 'picks up' and comments on or extends; **A** then responds to the comment or extension and **B** responds again and so on, passing the statement back and forth, developing it as they go along.

Variation
This can be done as a written rather than a verbal activity.

Zebra

The aim of this activity is to help pupils realise that there are some questions to which there are no clear cut answers and that in religious education we deal with a lot of these questions a lot of the time. It is a more sophisticated version of the Yes or No activity and can also be related to the Ultimate Questions exercise.

You will need for each group a piece of grey sugar paper or card. On the left hand side of this is stuck a white vertical band and on the right hand side a black vertical band. In between there is a grey area – the background sheet.

Sit pupils in groups of three or four around a table on which is placed the 'board'. Give them a set of 10–15 cards, prepared in advance with statements on them which require answers such as Yes or No, True or False, for example, 'Guru Nanak is the first Sikh Guru.' Explain that they have to place the 'correct answers' on the black band and the 'incorrect answers' on the white band. Each pupil then takes it in turn to pick up a card and place it where they think it should go. If one of their group thinks that they have misplaced the card they can move it when it comes to their turn, explaining why, but they then can't pick up another of the face-down cards until it is their turn again. When they have completed this set of cards and agreed that they are all on the right bands they are given a second set of 10–15 cards and asked to do the same with them. The second set, however, contain statements which need more subtle answers, or where personal preferences or beliefs affect the answer, for example, 'Going to the gurdwara is important.'

It shouldn't be long before pupils realise that it is not so easy to place some statements in either the black or the white bands but that the grey area might now be needed if they are ever to agree and so end the game.

Variation
Mix the two types of card up and ask them to place them on the black or white bands. How long does it take them before they realise there are two different types of questions here? What solutions do they offer?

Zoom Lens

On a large piece of paper draw four circles within circles – a bit like a 'bulls-eye' on a dartboard. The central circle represents 'The Most Important', the second 'Very Important', the third, 'Important' and the fourth 'Least Important'. This provides the framework for a clarification exercise. It can be used for thinking through issues such as bullying, crime and punishment or abortion. It can also be used for thinking about religious beliefs and practices such as factors which affect whether or not someone attends a place of worship. The activity acts as a zoom lens on a camera, bringing what is most important into 'close-up' view. Pupils have the picture but the activity helps them focus on the most important aspects.

Examples

The ten commandments
The ten commandments are each written out on different pieces of card. Pupils then in small groups decide where to place each one of them within the four circles. The outcome is completely left to them (they could put all of them in the 'Most Important' circle or all of them in the 'Least Important'). What matters is that they agree with their corporate decision and can give reasons for that decision.

Attitudes to drugs
Pupils devise twelve reasons why someone should not take drugs. They then prioritise these reasons as above.

What matters to Muslims
After a unit of work on Islam the teacher provides pupils with a series of statements about Islam. Pupils place these as they think a Muslim would.